Amelia Earhart

By Mary Nhin

Pictures By
Yuliia Zolotova

Hi, I'm Amelia Earhart.

I didn't have a very traditional childhood. In my day, little girls were supposed to wear dresses and behave 'nicely,' but my mother believed strongly in gender equality.

This dress might be a better option.
I like these overalls!
Yes, I like those on you, too, Amelia!

She dressed us in pants instead of skirts. She let us climb trees and catch frogs as we pleased.

I even built a little ramp on the shed roof and slid down it in a box. I got a lot of bruises, but to me it was exciting. It was my first taste of flying!

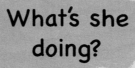

When I was old enough, I saved up for flying lessons by working, but it wasn't easy...

I arrived at the airfield for training, and I saw how few women there were there.

I was taught that you get in life what you have the courage to ask for.

I knew I was being judged for my feminine appearance, so I distressed my flying jacket to make me look more experienced. I cut my hair short, too.

When I finally finished my training, I was only the sixteenth woman in the U.S. to ever have obtained a pilot's license.

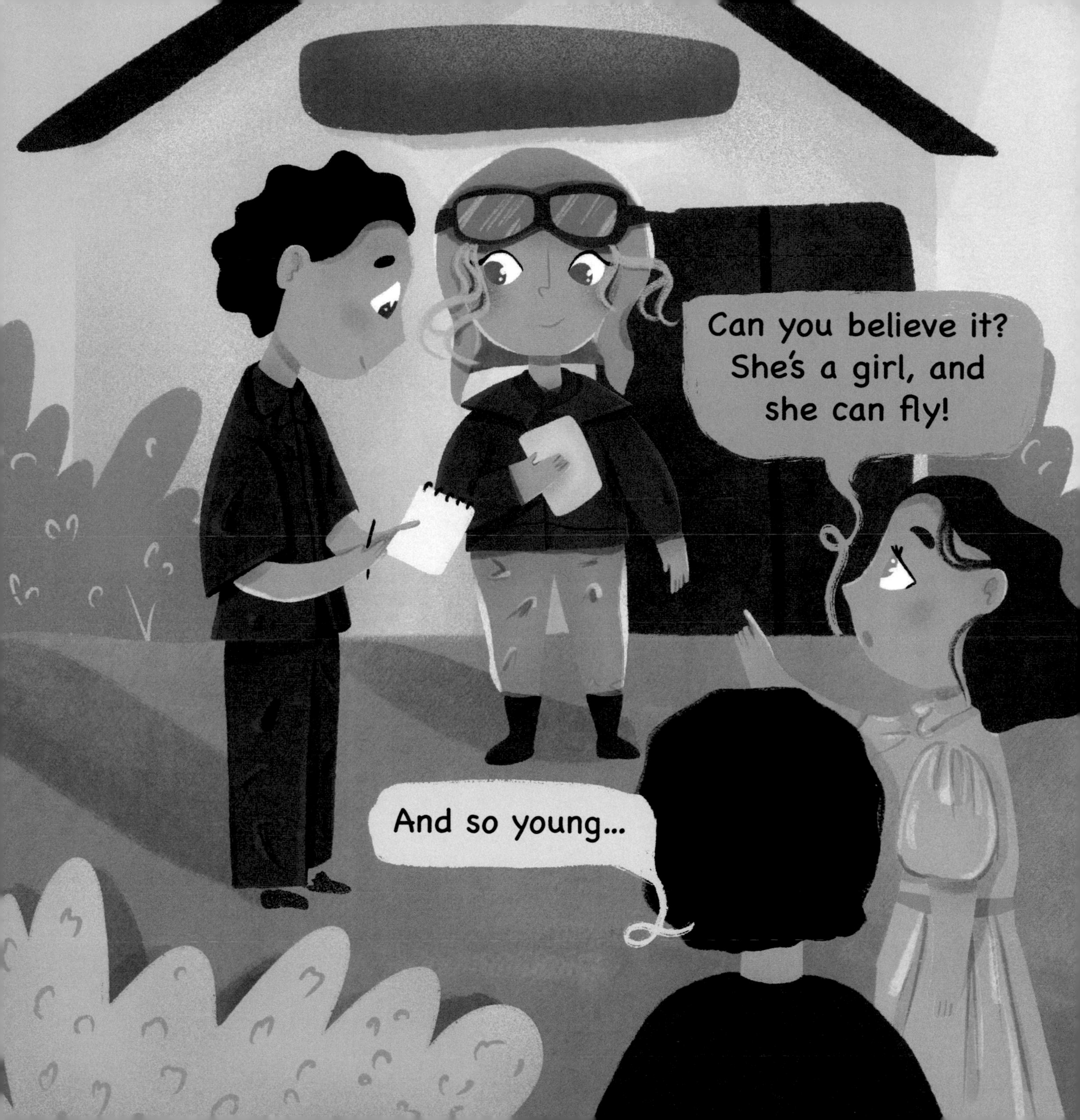
Can you believe it? She's a girl, and she can fly!
And so young...

My pioneering story almost ended there when I suffered from ill health.

When I ran out of money, I had to sell my plane. I even had to cancel my plans of going to university because I simply couldn't afford it.

I knew in my heart that if I wanted something, I had to work hard to get it. I began writing for papers and magazines to encourage more women to fly. This is how I earned a living as a writer and could afford to keep flying.

I worked hard to get here. I couldn't just give up. Even when no one else believed, I had to believe in myself.

Women must try to do things as men have tried. When they fail, their failure must be but a challenge to others.

I set my sights on the unknown, wanting to be one of the best pilots in history. I attempted dangerous feats never done before.

Never do things others can do and will do if there are things others cannot do or will not do.

I was the first woman to fly alone across the Atlantic Ocean, and I set lots of world records throughout my career.

I inspired many women in the US to achieve their dreams of flying just like I did. People had told me that I would fail, but I wasn't afraid to try.

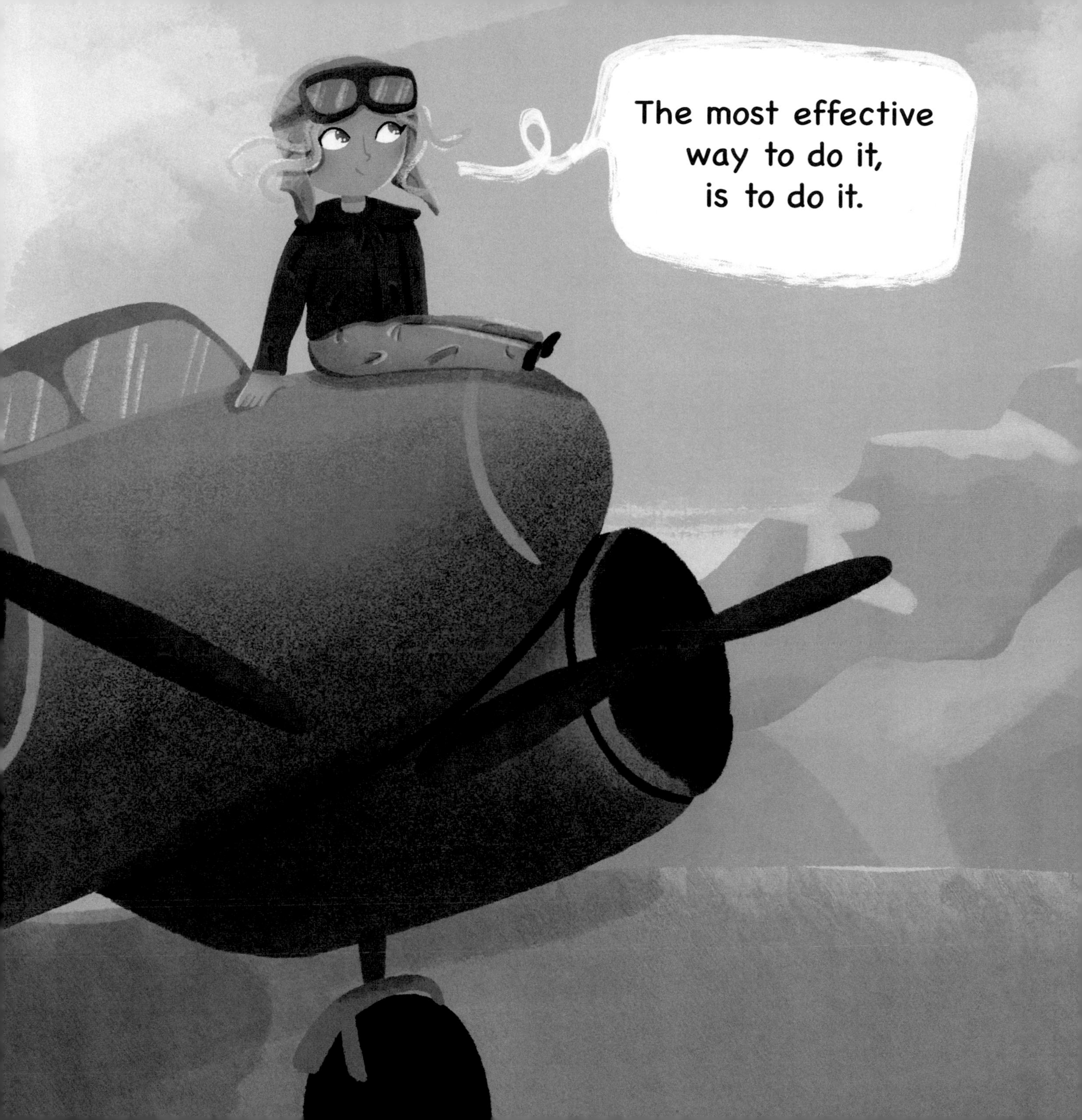
The most effective way to do it, is to do it.

Timeline

1923 – Amelia gets her pilot's license

1928 – Amelia becomes the first woman
to fly the Atlantic Ocean

1932 – Amelia becomes the first woman
to receive the Distinguished Flying Cross

1933 – Amelia becomes the first woman to
fly nonstop, coast-to-coast across the U.S.

 @marynhin   @GrowGrit
#minimoversandshakers

minimovers.tv

 Mary Nhin   Grow Grit

 Grow Grit

Made in the USA
Las Vegas, NV
30 April 2022

48209785R00021